W9-CCD-979

TRIUMPH
BOOKS

I Love You
2-11-12
Floralife
Crystal Clear

Remembering Whitney

The day after music superstar Whitney Houston was found dead in her room at the Beverly Hilton in Los Angeles, mourning fans left flowers, stuffed animals, and other items outside the hotel.

This book is available in quantity at special discounts for your group or organization.
For further information, contact:

Triumph Books LLC
542 South Dearborn Street
Suite 750
Chicago, IL 60605
Phone: (312) 939-3330
Fax: (312) 663-3557

www.triumphbooks.com

Printed in U.S.A.
ISBN: 978-1-60078-768-3

Content packaged by Mojo Media, Inc.
Joe Funk: Editor
Jason Hinman: Creative Director

All photos courtesy of Getty Images unless otherwise noted.

AP Images

Contents

The Day the Music Died

Above: A shirt featuring a photo of Whitney is seen in a makeshift memorial near the Beverly Hilton Hotel soon after she died. Opposite: Whitney sings on stage at Wembley Stadium in London during a June 1988 benefit concert for Nelson Mandela.

The news arrived suddenly, late in the afternoon on Saturday, February 11. Whitney Houston had been found, unresponsive, in her fourth-floor suite at the Beverly Hilton. Efforts to revive the singer failed, and the police pointed out that there were no signs of criminal intent. Whitney Houston was gone forever.

Coverage in the media world began almost instantly as her shocked fan base mourned and the stars began their tributes. Clive Davis, a longtime friend and host of the gala Houston was slated to attend that evening, turned his bash into an impromptu memorial to the singer. He spoke passionately about Houston during his opening remarks, becoming visibly emotional as he implored that the music play on, as Houston would have wanted.

The bash went off as planned, with Tony Bennett making a particularly notable speech. The singer had struggled with addiction in decades past, paying tribute to Houston while saying that she may well have been the best singer he had heard in his life. His touching performance of "How Do You Keep the Music Playing" moved all in attendance.

Other singers were quick to offer their condolences. Dolly Parton, who penned Houston's signature "I Will Always Love You" spoke graciously about her friend, taking near-reverential tones. Mariah Carey was also particularly moved.

AP Images

The news spread like wildfire. All of the major news networks broke from other coverage to cover Houston; the cable music channels immediately began airing Houston's old videos. Even sports channels deemed the event newsworthy, as her clip of "The Star Spangled Banner" at Super Bowl XXV immediately went into rotation.

Bobby Brown, estranged from his ex-wife for several years, was reportedly near hysterics at hearing the news. He performed within hours, toughing out an emotional night on stage during which he blew kisses to the sky while telling Whitney he loved her.

With the Grammys slated for Sunday, producers went into overdrive to pay tribute to the six-time winner, with Chaka Khan and Jennifer Hudson being tabbed to organize the live tribute. Having to walk a delicate line since the event was just one day removed from the Houston's passing, organizers knew the pair could pull off a respectful and incredible performance.

The show opened with a montage of Houston and a prayer from LL Cool J. After the roll call of artists who had passed away the year before, Hudson delivered the performance of the night with a show-stopping rendition of "I Will Always Love You".

The world may never know another singing talent quite like Houston. With an incredible pedigree and talented family to draw influence from, her rangy tones earned her the simple nickname of "The Voice". Few pop stars before or since could demonstrate the range Houston had, which rivaled that of the greatest opera singers.

Few artists could get away with what Whitney could thanks to her voice. So strong that it could stand alone as a true instrument, she was never shy about placing it front and center in her songs. None of her contemporaries in the 1980s or 1990s could match her range or vocal strength. Her voice inspired a rush of female pop singers with big voices, but none, not Mariah Carey, nor Celine Dion, could match the power Houston generated.

Her crossover appeal was unrivaled. No previous black female artist could sell records like Houston or draw the audiences she did. Her songs appealed to all, and her push to get on MTV cannot be understated in its importance. She paved the way for an entire class of pop star, and for that they will forever be indebted to Houston.

She always did things her way. On her debut full-length album, six of the songs were outright ballads, seemingly a disastrous choice in the big-everything 1980s. She stood tall and proud in the face of hard rock competition, creating her own genre of pop in the process.

The soul and gospel scenes always had their place in black America, but it had been years since the days of Mahalia Jackson and singers like Aretha Franklin were firmly planted in the pop category. Houston refused to let go of her roots, which may have further increased her popularity. She was revolutionary in her time; there was no one like Whitney. Though the imitators came in droves, they never could match the original.

Queen of the divas, Houston has served as an inspiration for nearly every female vocalist since. She was the best, and the numbers certainly back it up. In addition to her six Grammy Awards, Houston was honored with two Emmys. Her other achievements

Fans left signed cards, albums, flowers, and more outside the Beverly Hilton Hotel after Whitney's sudden death there on February 11, 2012.

Vietnamese fan ♡♡♡
We will alway love you...
Luôn nhớ Whitney mãi mãi
Love
13/2/12

LOVE

I Love You

To: Our Dear Whitney
from: the fans of Michael Jackson
We love you RIP!

A whole garden of flowers could not convey how much you are thought of each and every day

QUEEN OF POP GONE TO SOON
from
of Michael Jackson fans
.com

RIP Whitney!!
Thank You for all you have done.
You will not be forgotten ever!

I Love you Whitney, I know Michael loved you
Thank you so much for your life

Thank you so much
We love you
Russia ♡

* www.TEAMMICHAELJACKSON.com *

include 30 Billboard Music Awards (with 11 of those wins coming in 1994) and 22 American Music Awards. All told, she has been honored more than 400 times at awards ceremonies around the world.

Her albums have retained their critical success, with her debut featured on Rolling Stone's 500 Greatest Albums of All Time list and the Rock and Roll Hall of Fame's Definitive 200. Houston's incredible and meteoric rise to the top of the charts with her first album remains an unduplicated feat in music history.

All told, Houston has sold over 200 million albums and singles despite her relatively low album output. Only three women have outsold Houston in the United States, where she has sold an astonishing 55 million albums. There is no doubt that Whitney Houston changed the music industry. Her legacy as an innovator and a pioneer for black female singers is undisputed.

Houston was a success at everything she tried. Her live act was renowned for its display of her talents, her movie ventures were all box office hits, and her turns in television were always some of the highest rated performances or movies in their network's histories. It was no fluke that everything seemed to come up aces for Whitney Houston—she was a once in a lifetime talent. ❋

Fans Eric Williams, Travon Marshall, and others attended a vigil for Whitney at Leimert Park in Los Angeles two days after Houston died.

W H I T N E

Jennifer Hudson performs Whitney's signature song "I Will Always Love You" during a tribute to Whitney at the 54th Annual Grammy Awards.

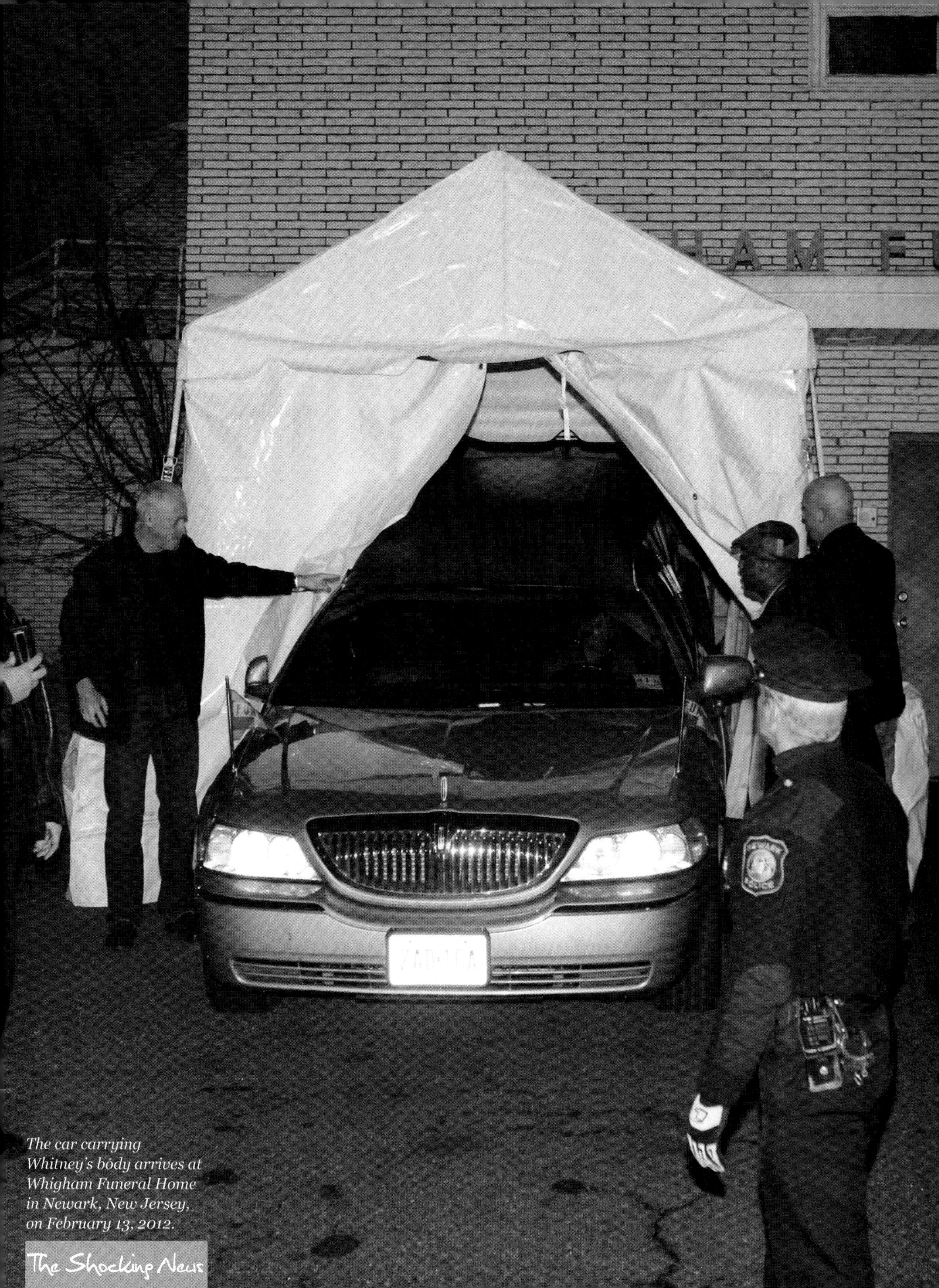

The car carrying Whitney's body arrives at Whigham Funeral Home in Newark, New Jersey, on February 13, 2012.

Ashanti and Terrence J participate in BET's 106 & Park tribute to Whitney.

106 AND PARK:
REMEMBERING
WHITNEY

The Early Years
The Voice and Looks of an Angel

Above: Record producer Clive Davis poses with a young Whitney after signing the budding star to her first recording contract with Arista Records in April 1983. Opposite: Whitney performs onstage in New York City in August 1987.

Born in a middle-class neighborhood in Newark, New Jersey, in 1963, Whitney Houston had music in her bones from the moment she left the womb. The youngest of Russell and Cissy Houston's three children, her music pedigree was second to none. Her mother was a fixture in the R&B, pop, and soul scenes, performing as a backup singer to artists including Elvis Presley, Mahalia Jackson, and Aretha Franklin. A cousin of Dionne and Dee Dee Warwick, young Whitney had a strong role model in Franklin, her godmother.

After moving around some to escape rioting in Newark, the Houston family settled down in East Orange, where 11-year-old Whitney began to sing. The New Hope Baptist Church's junior gospel choir had a true phenom on its hands, quickly making Houston its soloist. Records indicate that her first solo performance was the classic hymn "Guide Me, O Thou Great Jehovah." She also began to play her first musical instrument, the piano.

Taught primarily by her mother, it was clear that young Whitney had a special talent, perhaps even greater than Cissy herself. With her mother's singing as well as that of Franklin and the Warwicks, Whitney was exposed to some of the finest voices of the era. She also found influence from an early age

Clive Davis introduces a young, relatively unknown Whitney to fans in New York in 1984.

in the singing of artists like Gladys Knight, Roberta Flack, and Chaka Khan. She got to see superstardom firsthand: her cousin Dionne Warwick and godmother Aretha Franklin still stand as two of the most charted artists of all time.

As a teenager, Whitney met a person who changed her life: longtime best friend and executive assistant Robyn Crawford. While both attending Mt. Saint Dominic Academy, an all-girls school in Caldwell, the girls immediately formed a bond with one another that Houston always described as "sisterly".

Cissy was an active performer in the late 1970s, playing nightclubs throughout the Northeast with her daughter in tow. Whitney performed on stage with her mother on occasion, with ears drawn towards the adolescent with the big voice. At age 14 she performed on her first commercial track, singing backing vocals on the Michael Zager Band's single, "Life's a Party." Zager was impressed, offering to help Whitney obtain a recording contract. Cissy refused, saying that Whitney's education was more important.

This didn't stop young Whitney from singing. In 1978 at the age of 15, she backed up Chaka Khan on the singer's hit "I'm Every Woman", a song Whitney later covered. Singers such as Lou Rawls and the Jackson 5's Jermaine Jackson came calling for the teenager to sing on their records; her reputation was growing.

Whitney performs in New York in 1984. The next year, Houston would release her debut album, which sold more than 25 million albums and redefined the R&B genre.

Whitney performs with Jermaine Jackson during a rehearsal for the soap opera As the World Turns *in July 1984.*

AP Images

The Early Years

Whitney performs on stage in New York City in 1987. Only a few years removed from signing her first recording contract, by this time Whitney was a Grammy-winning artist with a best-selling debut album.

As the 1980s began, eyes were on Houston for a different reason: she was quite a beauty and the camera loved her. Modeling jobs in magazines such as *Cosmopolitan, Glamour,* and *Seventeen* made her one of the biggest teen models of the time; photographers and fans were drawn to her stunning looks and All-American personality.

She began to record songs as the lead vocalist as well. Contributing to an album credited to the band Material, Houston's ballad "Memories" was a highlight for critics and fans. Coveted by several record labels in the early part of the decade, Houston chose carefully. Arista head Clive Davis saw Houston in 1983 and offered her an international recording contract—Whitney was on her way to stardom.

National audiences saw Houston live for the first time when she appeared with Davis on the Merv Griffin Show later that year, but Whitney did not immediately start work on her first album. Instead, she earned her first top five R&B hit when she performed "Hold Me", a duet with Teddy Pendergrass.

February 1985 finally saw the debut of the album everyone was waiting for. Self-titled, Houston's first record earned rave reviews for the young singer. Her first single release established Houston as a star: the ballad "You Give Good Love" reached No. 3 on Billboard's Hot 100 while it topped the R&B chart.

Whitney, right, spends time with her mother Cissy Houston, center, and cousin Dionne Warwick after the 1987 American Music Awards.

AP Images

Whitney performs during a 1986 benefit concert at the Boston Garden. Over the next three decades, Whitney's charity work would generate millions of dollars for a variety of causes.

AP Images

Whitney performs at New York's Madison Square Garden in September 1987.

All of the sudden, Houston was in demand on the nightclub and television scene. Her next single release was even bigger; the jazzed-up "Saving All My Love for You" topped the charts in the United States and United Kingdom. Touring with Jeffrey Osborne as her hits rocketed up the charts, Houston was becoming a bigger star than the man she was opening for.

MTV's audience got their first taste of Houston with the video for "How Will I Know," another No. 1 hit. She became the first black female mainstay in the channel's rotation. By 1986, *Whitney Houston* was on top of the album charts, eventually logging 14 weeks in the top spot. A third No. 1 hit was scored with "Greatest Love of All", making her the first woman to land three songs in the top spot on her debut album.

Winning her first Grammy in 1986, Houston was an instant star thanks to the power of *Whitney Houston,* a dream beginning for any artist. Expectations were high as 1987 rolled around and Houston's second album, *Whitney,* was on the way.

Not deviating much from the formula that made Houston's first album a success, *Whitney* debuted at No. 1 on the album chart, making her the first woman to accomplish the feat. Whitney's first single, "I Wanna Dance with Somebody [Who Loves Me]" was her biggest hit to date, peaking at No. 1 all over the world. Houston's next three singles

Whitney performs during a concert London's Wembley Arena in May 1988. Inset: Whitney poses with her two American Music Awards in 1989. She was named Favorite Pop/Rock Female Artist and Favorite R&B/Soul Female Artist.

The Early Years

Whitney, right, poses with Elizabeth Taylor, Lisa Minelli, and Michael Jackson at a New York event in 1988.

all reached No. 1 on the Hot 100, giving Houston seven straight singles in the top spot, breaking a record held by the Bee Gees and Beatles.

Touring internationally and becoming one of music's biggest earners because of it, there was little doubt that Whitney Houston was on the pop scene to stay. "I Wanna Dance With Somebody" won Houston another Grammy and ran the table at other awards shows.

Houston turned her attention to giving back as the 1980s drew to an end. A firm supporter of Nelson Mandela and the South African anti-apartheid movement, Houston joined a star-studded lineup in London to raise over $1 million dollars for charities while raising awareness about the imprisoned Mandela and apartheid. Another charity concert in New York raised $250,000 for the United Negro College Fund.

Motivated by her charitable work, Houston formed her own non-profit in 1989, The Whitney Houston Foundation For Children. Caring for the homeless and sick while also giving them tools for success, the charity became an important part of Houston's life. She had been a backing singer when the decade started, but by the end of the 1980s Houston's popularity rivaled that of any pop star in the world. ✻

Whitney (second from right) shares a moment with her mother Cissy Houston (right), boxing promoter Don King, and cousin Dionne Warwick in 1987.

The 1990s
A Pop Queen Reigns Supreme

Above: Whitney performs with her cousin, Dionne Warwick. Opposite: Whitney performs at a New York concert in the early 1990s. The energy she brought to her music was a key to her success.

As the 1990s began, Whitney Houston was as much a household name as any other star in the music business. She had a strong start to the decade, seen by the entire country on January 27, 1991, when she sang the national anthem before Super Bowl XXV in Tampa. Considered by many to be the definitive version of "The Star Spangled Banner," Houston wowed the nation. The single version of the song became the highest-charting rendition of the national anthem ever during its initial release. Houston donated all of the proceeds to the Red Cross, earning her a seat on its board.

Sung during a time of great unrest with war underway in the Persian Gulf, the national anthem earned Houston respect from all corners. Later that year, she worked with HBO to produce the Welcome Home Heroes concert, a free show for 3,500 veterans. The highest rated show in HBO's history to that point, the concert further cemented Houston's patriotic credentials.

Whitney took big steps in her personal life in the early 1990s, as well. After being romantically linked with multiple celebrities in the 1980s, she had seemingly found love at the end of the decade with R&B singer Bobby Brown. The two married in July of

The 1990s

Whitney, left, performs a duet with CeCe Winans at the 1996 Grammy Awards.

AP Images

The 1990s

Whitney added acting to her résumé in the 1990s. Here she is seen with James Woods (left) and Richard Dreyfuss.

1992, with Houston giving birth to her only child, Bobbi Kristina, the next year.

With success as a singer and model, Houston decided to try another creative avenue in 1992. She made her acting debut as a music superstar being stalked by a crazed fan opposite Kevin Costner in 1992's *The Bodyguard.* One of the most memorable films of the year, it was a huge success at the box office, grossing more than $410 million worldwide.

Even more notable than the film was its soundtrack. Produced by Houston and featuring six of her songs, the soundtrack was an international smash hit. No. 1 on the album chart for 20 weeks, it sold a million copies in the week before Christmas, the first album to sell that many copies in a week since tracking began.

Though there were other notable tracks on the album, one in particular stood out. A No. 1 country hit for Dolly Parton in the 1970s, the track "I Will Always Love You" was initially a second choice for the album. Included when another potential cover was included in a different movie, "I Will Always Love You" became a smash hit, as well as Houston's signature song.

Topping the Hot 100 for a then-record 14 weeks straight, the song was a hit all over the world. The best selling single by a woman

A beaming Houston sits down with President George Bush in 1990. Perhaps the biggest pop star in the world as the 1990s began, Houston was a draw for the common man and presidents alike.

Whitney Houston reaches out for 7-month old Hector Nieves, who suffers from chronic lung disease, during a visit to Miami's Ronald McDonald House.

AP Images

Perhaps at her live peak, Whitney sings in concert in Miami in 1991.

The 1990s

The 1990s

In perhaps Whitney's single most memorable performance, she sang the national anthem before Super Bowl XXV in 1991. Her rendition of "The Star Spangled Banner" became a rallying cry during the first World War and was a chart-topping single.

in the United States at the time, it sold 12 million copies worldwide. By the time its run was over, the song had topped the chart for 20 total weeks, another record. Her next two singles reached the top five while "I Will Always Love You" was still selling strong, making Houston the first woman to ever have three songs in the top 11 of the singles chart at the same time. The soundtrack ended up selling 44 million copies worldwide, making it one of the top 10 best-selling albums ever.

Houston's performance on the soundtrack won her three Grammys in 1994, including the prestigious Album of the Year and Record of the Year. As usual, she cleaned up at the other award shows before going back on an all-encompassing world tour, a hallmark of Houston's career. Her stretch from 1993 to 1994 was nearly unrivaled as only two women, Oprah Winfrey and Barbara Streisand, were higher female earners in the entertainment business.

She saw one of her dreams realized later in 1994, as Nelson Mandela—released from prison as South Africa liberalized—was elected president of the country and dismantled the apartheid system. Houston was invited to attend a state dinner at the White House in Mandela's honor. She later traveled to South Africa to perform in front of more than 200,000 people over three concerts. All proceeds were donated to South African charities.

Whitney and Kevin Costner share a lighthearted moment on the set of The Bodyguard. *The film was Whitney's breakout performance as an actress and the movie's soundtrack was one of her most successful albums.*

The 1990s

Whitney's success in screen and song provided a life of luxury. Her expansive New Jersey home that she shared with then-husband Bobby Brown and daughter Bobbi Kristina is pictured from the air in 1993.

Whitney greets Muhammad Ali on stage as the former boxing champion accepts a GQ "Men of the Year" award in 1998.

AP Images

Whitney was a favorite in Europe throughout her career. She is seen here performing in Paris during her 1993 world tour.

Houston continued to act in the mid-1990s, appearing next in 1995's *Waiting to Exhale*, playing the lead role of a television producer who falls for a married man. The movie opened at No. 1 at the box office while Houston earned rave reviews for pushing herself as an actress. The soundtrack was produced by Houston and Babyface, with Houston's main contribution "Exhale (Shoop Shoop)" giving her another number one hit. The album was critically acclaimed and hit number one on the album charts.

The singer stayed on the big screen the next year, appearing opposite Denzel Washington in *The Preacher's Wife*. By now one of the highest-paid actresses in Hollywood, Houston was again critically acclaimed for her performance in the successful film, earning award nominations.

Another soundtrack album produced by Houston followed, selling six million copies. Consisting of gospel music, it became the highest-selling album ever in the genre. Praised for its emotional caliber, it displayed a new side of Houston's singing talent.

A turn on the small screen followed in 1997, as Houston starred in a made-for-television version of Cinderella. Starring as the fairy godmother and with her company producing the movie, Houston saw her television movie debut earn ABC some of its highest ratings ever while garnering seven Emmy nominations.

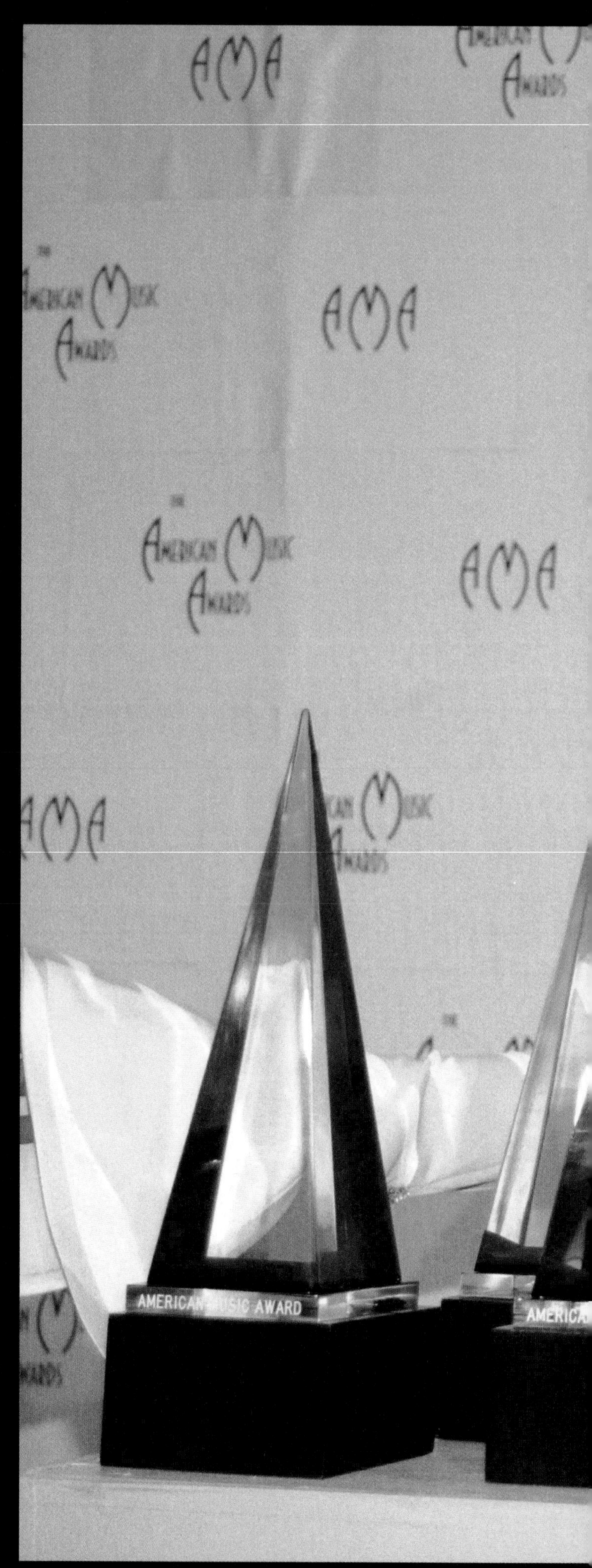

The awards shows rarely overlooked Houston. Here she cannot contain her excitement as she poses with her six-trophy haul at the 1994 American Music Awards.

THE AMERICAN MUSIC AWARDS
AMA
AMERICAN MUSIC AWARD
AMERICAN MUSIC AWARD
AMERICAN MUSIC AWARD

Proud parents Whitney and Bobby Brown pose with their only child, the infant Bobbi Kristina, in 1993.

The 1990s

The biggest sports event in the world deserved the biggest pop star in the world. Whitney performs here before 100,000 fans at the 1994 World Cup final at the Rose Bowl.

Despite adding the titles of "actress" and "mother" to her growing résumé in the 1990s, Whitney continued to tour and pack arenas worldwide.

Whitney Houston and husband Bobby Brown enjoy a moment together during the 1995 MTV Video Music Awards in New York.

Though she had spent several years acting and working on soundtracks, a return to the studio was in the cards for Houston. *My Love Is Your Love,* her first studio effort in eight years, came out in November 1998. Originally slated to be a greatest hits compilation with some new tracks, the recording sessions proved so fruitful that Houston went ahead with a full new album. Recorded in just six weeks, it saw Houston pushing her boundaries to include funk and other urban styles. "When you Believe", a duet with Mariah Carey, won an Academy Award after being featured in the movie *The Prince of Egypt.* Overall, the album was critically acclaimed as Whitney sang with unbridled passion.

As the decade drew to a close, there was no doubt that Houston was still the premier female singer in the world. She had success in everything she attempted throughout the decade, making her a movie star, an acclaimed producer, and the highest-selling R&B artist of all time. ✻

Whitney and Mariah Carey, left, present the award for Best Male Video during the 1998 MTV Video Awards.

AP Images

Whitney performs "Until You Come Back to Me" during the 1999 American Music Awards.

The 1990s

AP Images

Whitney is seen smiling as she receives one of the most touching honors of her career. She was attending a ceremony at the former Franklin School in her hometown of East Orange, New Jersey as it was renamed the Whitney E. Houston Academy of Creative and Performing Arts.

Whitney performs "It's Not Right, But It's Okay" at the 1999 Soul Train Music Awards.

The 1990s

One of the artists that followed directly in Whitney's footsteps, Janet Jackson smiles as she sits alongside Whitney at a party for the Elton John AIDS Foundation in the run up to the Academy Awards. Jackson owed a major debt of gratitude to Houston, a true trailblazer in the 1980s.

The 1990s

Whitney debuts a new look in February 1999 when she takes the stage to perform at the BRIT Awards in London. A true global superstar, she enjoyed some of her biggest record sales in Great Britain.

Mary J. Blige watches as Whitney belts out her portion of their duet at the 1999 VH1 Divas Concert in New York.

The 2000s
Entering a New Era

Above: Big smiles and happy days seemed to be the rule for Whitney and husband, Bobby Brown, when they appeared at the 2000 MTV Video Music Awards in New York. Opposite: A six-time Grammy winner, Whitney was no stranger to music's biggest night. At the 2000 ceremony, she performed a pair of hits from her album My Love is Your Love.

After a two-decade run that saw Whitney become one of the biggest stars in the world, the 2000s were to represent a whole new set of challenges for the talented artist. Starting the new millennium as a true superstar, the weight of that crown was to become heavy as a long, hardworking touring career began to catch up to her.

She began the decade with the greatest hits album she had been meaning to release two years before. *Whitney: The Greatest Hits* reached No. 1 overseas and peaked in the top five in the United States, yet another hit album. Her signature ballads were left unchanged for the record, but several of the up-tempo numbers were remixed. The package included several bonuses, such as new songs, non-album tracks and a DVD that featured live performances and videos. It was a major success, selling 10 million copies worldwide.

As her professional career stayed as strong as ever, whispers began to circulate about Houston and Brown's personal struggles. A pair of award show cancellations further fueled the rumors, and her live performances seemed to suffer. Robyn Crawford, a mainstay in Houston's life and an important part of her team, quit in 2001.

None of the questions about her life seemed to faze Whitney. In August 2001 she signed the richest contract in music history with Arista—a $100 million deal for six new albums, plus a generous royalty

The 2000s

A rare sight as Michael Jackson and Whitney share the stage to perform at the Miracle on 34th Street concert in New York City in 2000. The pair had run side by side as two of the most vital pop singers of the 1980s and 1990s but performed together infrequently.

Whitney can't hide her joy as friend, Kenneth "Babyface" Edmonds, presents the pop star her Lifetime Achievement trophy at the very first BET Awards in 2001.

Whitney sang "Wanna Be Startin' Something" at the Michael Jackson 30th Anniversary Celebration in 2001.

payment plan. Houston rounded out the year with an appearance at the 30th anniversary spectacular for Michael Jackson and another Top 10 hit when her rendition of the national anthem made it to No. 6 on the charts in the wake of the 9/11 terrorist attacks. As she had on numerous occasions throughout the years, Houston donated the proceeds to charity.

Earnestly preparing for her new record in 2002, Houston was in demand on the interview scene. Looking to promote her newest studio effort, the upcoming *Just Whitney…*, the singer appeared on television with Diane Sawyer. The highest rated television interview in history was gripping. Houston admitted to past drug use but was adamantly in denial of the rumors around her life at the time, speaking forcefully on the topic.

Her fifth studio album was her first without Clive Davis producing, with her husband, Missy Elliott, and Babyface taking over the duties. It was another huge hit, scoring Houston her highest-selling debut week ever. The singles to the album were well-received but did not replicate Houston's earlier chart success, though the album itself sold 3 million copies around the world.

The next year saw the release of Houston's first Christmas album, *One Wish: The Holiday Album.* Featuring traditional holiday songs and arrangements, it was a success with the public and critics alike, yielding a hit with "One Wish (For Christmas)". Houston was on the road with a vengeance throughout 2003-2004, touring all over Europe, Asia, the Middle East and Russia.

The envy of women everywhere in 2001, Whitney shares a lighthearted kiss with Usher during the Michael Jackson 30th Anniversary Celebration, Just months earlier, she had signed the richest contract in music history—$100 million for six new albums.

The 2000s

Whitney recognized the power of performing her music on television and remained a fixture on the small screen throughout her career. In December 2002, she recorded a live performance at New York's Lincoln Center for Good Morning America.

Whitney partnered with one of her frequent collaborators, Mary J. Blige, at the 2002 VH1 Divas show in Las Vegas. The pair sang "Rainy Dayz."

An emotional reunion with Davis came at the 2004 World Music Awards, with the singer paying tribute to her longtime friend. After the show, the two announced plans to work together on Houston's next album, news that rocked the pop world and marking an important reunion for the hit-making team.

Meanwhile, Houston's husband Bobby Brown tried to revive his career with a new television series, *Being Bobby Brown.* The show was set to center around Houston's husband, but since it chronicled his personal life, Houston ended up with just as much screen time as her husband. The domestic angle and some creative editing by the producers painted Houston in a less than flattering light, and the show was critically panned. It was a smash with the public, however, as it yielded high ratings for the Bravo network and signaled yet another success for Houston in a non-music performance.

Years of tumult had taken its toll on the marriage, and it showed in screen. The couple was at the end of the line, separating in September 2006. Their divorce went quickly, finalizing early the next year, though legal battles continued after, with Houston coming out on top.

After losing her way from her career in the middle of the decade, Houston came back with a vengeance as it came toward its close. Interviewed for the first time in seven years when she appeared on the Oprah Winfrey Show in September 2009, Houston was remarkably candid in revealing her personal demons and struggles with Brown.

Rumors swirled about Houston's personal life but she managed to dodge most questions during the early 2000s. Always able to get herself up to perform, she sings here for a television special in 2002 at the Lincoln Center in New York.

AP Images

Opposite: Whitney was the picture of elegance in October 2006 as she arrived at the 17th Carousel of Hope Ball in Beverly Hills.

No matter the struggles in her personal life, Whitney always looked good on stage. This outfit turned heads at the 2002 European Music Awards in Spain.

The 2000s

VH1's Divas Duets showcased some of the best singing voices of all time. Houston can't contain a big smile as she performs with one of the legends of music, Stevie Wonder.

A cathartic experience for the signer, she was back in the spotlight as well.

Her new album, *I Look To You,* was a return to Houston's superstardom of a decade before. Debuting at No. 1 on the album charts, it was her first top record since the soundtrack to The Bodyguard and her first pure studio No. 1 since 1987. Promoting the album at home and abroad, Houston was singing with a vigor not seen in several years. The album went platinum, a remarkable feat in the new digital era of music.

It seemed like Houston was on the road to a remarkable comeback, and coming in year that saw Michael Jackson succumb to his myriad health issues well before his time, it was a welcome feel-good story in the pop world. Always a star on the touring circuit, Houston prepared to head out on a world tour.

The Nothing But Love world tour was even more expansive than her last, an ambitious effort that looked to touch all corners of the world. Billed as Houston's triumphant return to the top, it did not quite see Houston at her best. Struggling to get her live voice back in its entirety and worn out from the strain of the heavy schedule, the tour was not as successful as her previous ones had been.

There had certainly been ups and downs for Houston in the 2000s. Her personal life had dominated the media coverage of the singer as she remained as big of a seller as ever. With her problems now seemingly in the rearview mirror and a successful album and long tour underway, it looked like Whitney Houston was ready for another decade atop the charts. ❋

Whitney's marriage to Bobby Brown seemed like a true musical love story during the happier times. Here the stylishly matching couple performs together at the 2003 VH1 Divas Duets benefit concert in Las Vegas.

"The Voice" never left Whitney. Still belting out notes she could hit 20 years before, Houston performs at the 2004 World Music Awards in Las Vegas.

The 2000s

Whitney offered a stunning performance at the 2009 American Music Awards in Los Angeles, proving that she still reigned as one of the world's greatest entertainers.

AP Images

Opposite: Clive Davis' annual pre-Grammy bash was always one of the biggest social events on Whitney's calendar. This photo was taken before the 2008 party at the Beverly Hilton, the same place where tragedy struck the singer just four years later.

Two generations of talent come together at Clive Davis' 2008 pre-Grammy party. Alicia Keys has never been shy about citing Whitney as an important influence on her career.

The Queen of Pop takes the stage with The Greatest in 2008. The gala affair, Muhammad Ali's Celebrity Fight Night XIV, raises money for Parkinson's research.

The 2000s

Always comfortable and radiant when performing, Whitney knew how to captivate an audience. In 2009 she took the stage for a stunning live performance during the popular German television show Wetten Dass.

The 2000s

As a former model, Whitney knew how to wow at awards shows—like here, at the 2009 Grammys—with her stunning looks and fashionable gowns.

The 2000s

Singer Whitney Houston, right, sings with her daughter Bobbi Kristina Brown during a performance for Good Morning America *in Central Park on Tuesday, Sept. 1, 2009 in New York.*

AP Images

The 2010s
Returning to Form

Above: In support of her album I Look To You, *Whitney embarked on an expansive world tour in 2010. This show was in May in Berlin in front of a full house. Opposite: Whitney Houston performs at the pre-Grammy gala and salute to industry icons with Clive Davis honoring David Geffen in February 2011, in Beverly Hills.*

Beginning the new decade on tour, things were looking up for Houston as 2010 began. Though the tour was marred by some uneven performances and snarky reviews, Houston was still obviously comfortable on the stage. Always a tour de force in person, she tried to finish the tour strong despite her mounting exhaustion.

Houston was back in the conversation for awards in January of the year, earning a pair of nominations at the NAACP Image Awards, taking home the trophy for Best Music Video for "I Look to You". An MTV pioneer nearly three decades before, Houston had always taken care to release music videos that were well-made and well-received.

Recognized as a pioneer and a queen of the pop world, other artists began to pay tribute to Houston. One notable performance came thanks to the strength of Jennifer Hudson and Kate Burrell performing at the BET Honors celebration, earning the singers rave reviews as they singled out Houston's music. Without Whitney Houston, after all, the black female pop singer as we know it may have never existed. She had paved the way for Janet Jackson, Mariah Carey, and Hudson, along with countless other talented singers that might have been held back by their race and gender before Houston came on the scene.

On the heels of a strong album and with the critics taking notice that Whitney Houston was far from finished as an artist, she announced her intention to

AP Images

Whitney Houston performs with Dionne Warwick at the pre-Grammy gala and salute to industry icons with Clive Davis honoring David Geffen in February 2011, in Beverly Hills.

AP Images

make a new record. Musing about her eighth studio effort, she said she wanted to work with the Black Eyed Peas' will.i.am, a notable producer and collaborator in his own right.

Houston performed at awards shows and special events once her tour was over, taking in a German Echo Awards celebration and performing "I Look to You" with gospel singer Kim Burrell at the January, 2011, BET Celebration of Gospel. She continued on the scene in the early part of the year, singing in tribute to her cousin Dionne Warwick at Clive Davis' annual pre-Grammy event.

Still battling her long-time struggles with substance abuse, in May 2011 Houston enrolled in an outpatient rehabilitation program to help kick drugs and alcohol for good. The program seemed to accelerate Houston's recovery process, and she emerged from the summer ready to get back to work.

In September, it was reported that Houston was to appear alongside Mike Epps and Jordin Sparks in a remake of the 1976 movie *Sparkle.* Slated to play the mother of Sparks' main character, Houston was also attached as a producer, a role she had performed with aplomb in the past. The role was set to stretch Houston's acting chops—the mother in the film is not encouraging, even disparaging, towards her talented daughter.

Houston had been attached to the project for 10 years, obtaining the production rights to the remake and tabbing singer Aaliyah to take the lead role. Aaliyah's tragic death in a plane crash in 2001 halted preproduction on

Whitney Houston performs at the pre-Grammy gala and salute to industry icons with Clive Davis honoring David Geffen in February 2011, in Beverly Hills.

AP

the film, throwing it into limbo. Excited about this passion project, it was seen as a major development in Houston's career now that it was back on track.

Still in the midst of her $100 million deal with Arista, Houston was dealt a blow to her recording career when Arista, the only label she had ever known, was disbanded by parent RCA Music Group. The conglomerate shut down several successful labels in the broad stroke, assuming the rights to any of Houston's future studio work.

Unfortunately, the singer never lived to see what life on a new label would look like. With her music career still going strong and new movie project she was very excited for, things looked like they were only going up for Houston as 2012 began.

In Los Angeles for the Grammys, Houston was slated to make her annual appearance at Davis' gala affair. She spent time early in February visiting with a pair of young singers, the talented Brandy and Monica, at rehearsals for the event. The day Houston died, she made her last appearance, joining Kelly Price on stage at the rehearsal, working on their duet of "Yes, Jesus Loves Me." Described as being a little off in her personality, Houston retired to her hotel after nearly 30 years of hit making, producing and acting that had made her undoubtedly one of the music industry's biggest stars ever. ✻

Whitney thrills a German audience in May 2010 during her worldwide Nothing But Love tour—a comeback tour that, sadly, was the singer's last.

AP Images

WHITNEY HOUSTON
COMPACT
disc
DIGITAL AUDIO

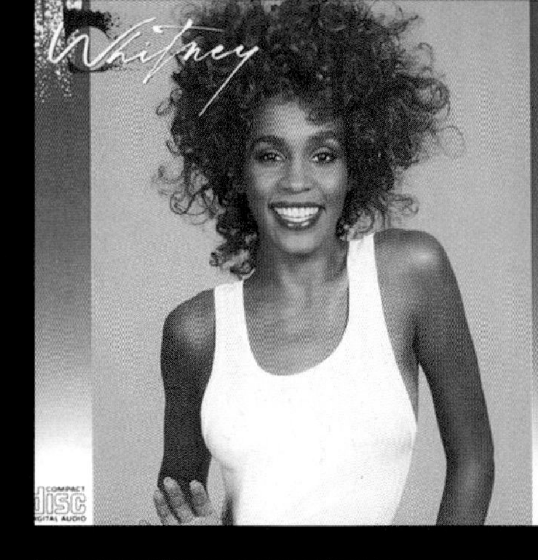
Whitney
COMPACT
disc
DIGITAL AUDIO

Whitney Houston
NIPPY
I'm Your Baby Tonight

Whitney Houston
The Preacher's Wife
ORIGINAL SOUNDTRACK ALBUM

JUST WHITNEY...

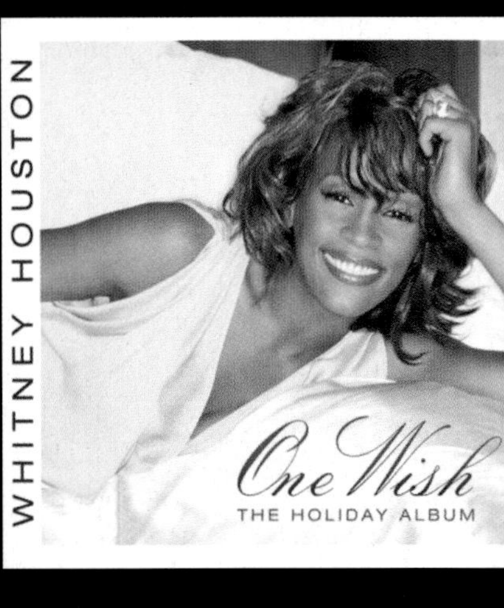
WHITNEY HOUSTON
One Wish
THE HOLIDAY ALBUM

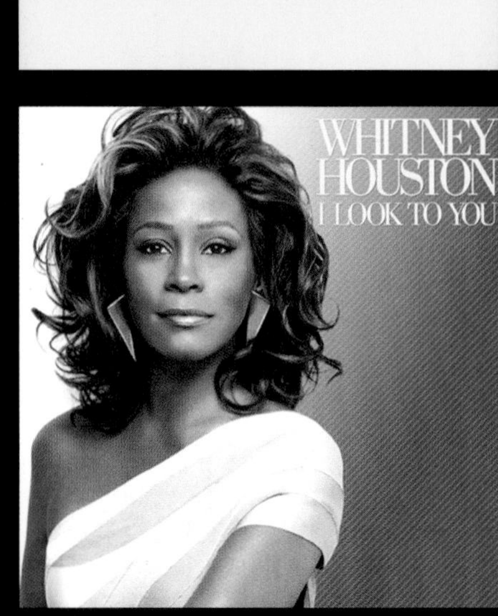
WHITNEY
HOUSTON
I LOOK TO YOU

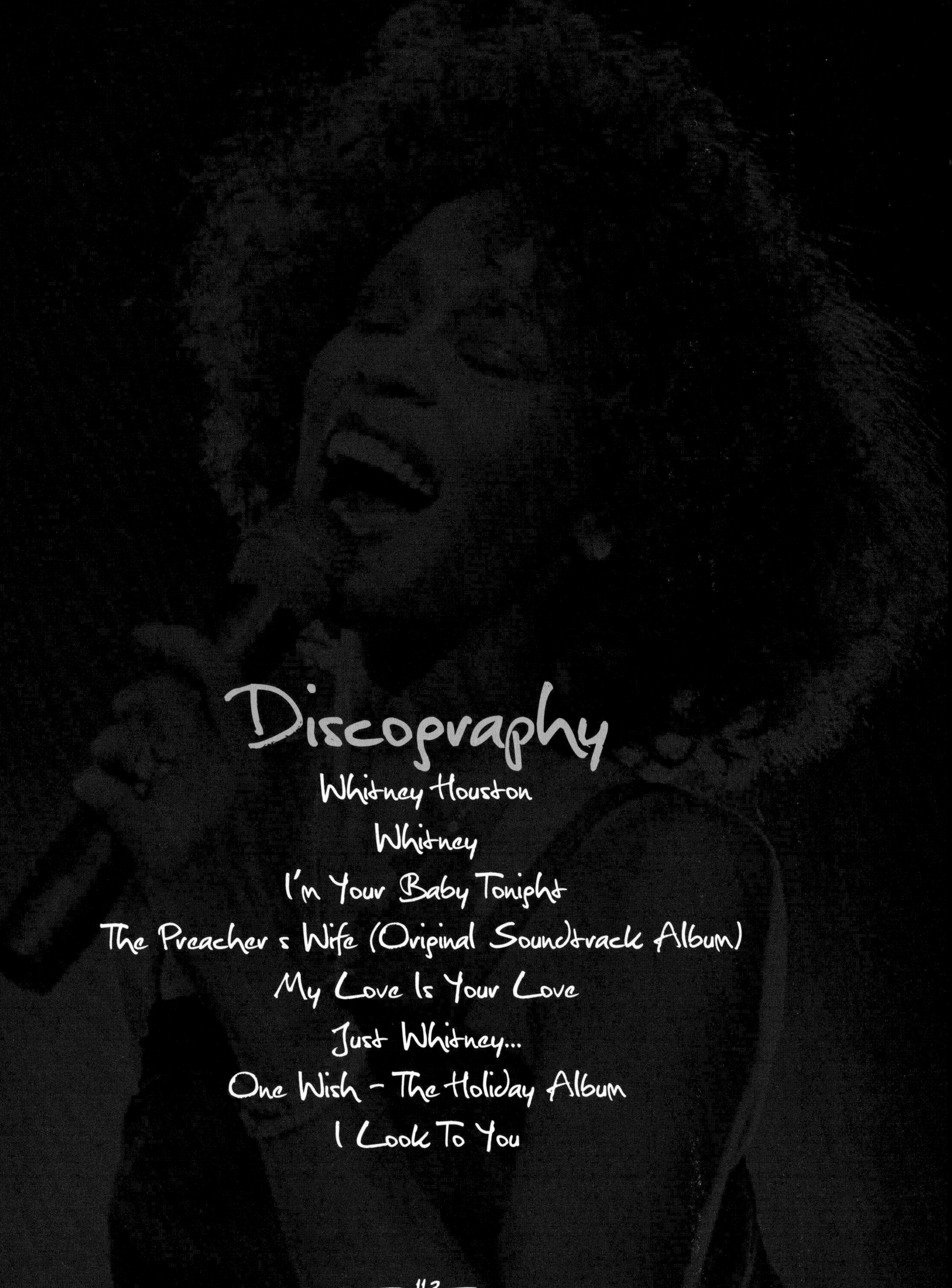

Discography

Whitney Houston

Whitney

I'm Your Baby Tonight

The Preacher's Wife (Original Soundtrack Album)

My Love Is Your Love

Just Whitney...

One Wish - The Holiday Album

I Look To You

So Long Whitney

"Whitney Houston was the first CD I ever bought. She had a God given gift. Hopefully, she's singing with angels now. I can't stop crying. I have a show to do soon. Wow, I learned how to do what I do because of 3 great women, one being Whitney. She was always so kind to me. This is not gonna be an easy show for sure. I'm doing what she taught me to do by listening to her records over and over as a little girl. Her death is very surreal."

LeAnn Rimes

"I feel sick.... Life is precious, we are fragile souls. Let's love each other! I miss you beautiful Whitney, the whole world misses you!!"

Alicia Keys

AP Images

"This is the saddest thing I've ever had to write in my life, RIP to one of the greatest humans that I have ever known Whitney Houston"
Wyclef Jean

"Such a loss. One of the greatest voices of our time. Sending out prayers to her family... RIP Whitney."

Jennifer Lopez

"I am so sad to hear about Whitney. We have lost one of the greatest singers of all time."

Simon Cowell

"We have lost another legend. Love and prayers to Whitney's family. She will be missed."

Christina Aguilera

"I'm distraught over the news that Whitney Houston has died! She was the most INCREDIBLE talent. What another sad day for the world."

Latoya Jackson

"I found my voice singing Whitney Houston's music. Today I lost my idol."

Jessica Simpson

"RIP Whitney Houston, really can't believe this"

Russell Simmons

"Oh Dear Lord! Huritng so Bad!!! MY Sister Whitney!!!!!!! Newark please Pray!!! World Please Pray!"

Queen Latifah

"Cookie and I are shocked and saddened about the news of Whitney Houston. A great friend and one of the most beautiful voices this world"
Earvin Magic Johnson

"RIP Whitney. So sad."

John Legend

"I'm so sad…Whitney Houston was so kind, sweet, wonderful, amazing, talented, and a true gift to the world…"

will.i.am

"RIP Whitney Houston dead at 48. Music is forever though"

Young Jeezy

"My heartfelt condolences to Whitney's family and to all her millions of fans throughout the world. She will never be forgotten as one of the greatest voices to ever grace the earth."

Mariah Carey

"It's a tragedy. Whitney Houston was the greatest singer I've ever heard and she will be truly missed."

Tony Bennett

"just heard the news. so crazy. One of the GREATEST VOICES EVER just passed. RIP Whitney Houston. My prayers go out to her friends and family"

Justin Bieber

In a rare studio shot, Houston records alongside Mariah Carey for the soundtrack to The Prince of Egypt. *Their duet "When You Leave" proved to be a smash hit, winning the singers – and producer Babyface – an Academy Award for Best Original Song.*

AP Images

"Tell our loved ones how much we love them while they're still here. I wish I could've told Whitney how great she was one last time"

Nick Cannon

"My heart is weeping...RIP to the Legendary Diva and Icon Whitney Houston!!!!! Such an incredible influence over music as a whole!"

Toni Braxton

"Rest in Peace Whitney We are heartbroken. She had the voice of an angel and a true artist's soul. Our deep love..."

Heart

"I just can't talk about it now. It's so stunning and unbelievable. I couldn't believe what I was reading coming across the TV screen."

Aretha Franklin

"So devastating. We will always love you Whitney, RIP"

Katy Perry

Producer Narada Michael Walden poses in 1989 with two of music's biggest superstars—Whitney Houston and her godmother, Aretha Franklin. The singers were in Detroit to record a historic duet, the single "It Isn't, It Wasn't, It Ain't Never Gonna Be."

The Greatest Love of All